The Opiate
Books

"Addiction begins with the hope that something 'out there' can instantly fill up the emptiness inside."

-Jean Kilbourne

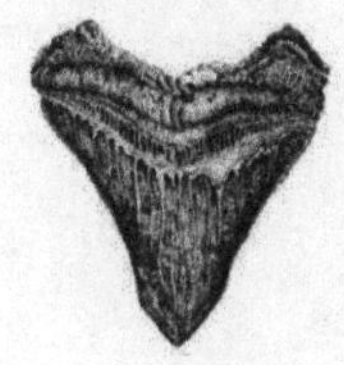

Table of Contents

Table of Contents

Foreword

Like many of the writers who make contact with *The Opiate*, Donna Dallas seemed to materialize from some divine ether. Her first published poem in one of our print issues, "Closed for Renovation," appeared in the ninth volume of the magazine. That was back in the spring of 2017, and it featured a particularly polarizing cover (i.e., a giant dildo surrounded by Barbie heads and other assorted Barbie parts…some attached to the heads, some not—you just never know what's going to scandalize people these days). Donna was among the few contributors who didn't shy away from the sudden "controversy" once the cover was unveiled. In addition to her poetry itself and how it affected me, I knew that her "so what" attitude about this particular image was the moment she solidified herself in my eyes as that rare breed in the twenty-first century: a True Artist (in other words, someone who understands the difference between freedom of expression and "being offensive"). With her second poetry collection, *Megalodon*, I am struck by what a gift it has been to read her work over the years and watch it evolve while remaining steadfastly "fuck you." Just like that volume nine issue she first showed up in.

As for the title of this book, when we think of a megalodon, we imagine it as a mythic creature. A shark-like creature, sure—but still a mythic one. Even though it was real, its extinction has made it "the stuff of legend," so to speak. Which is what each and every person's life will become once they're gone. Some far too soon. With only those few left behind able to rehash the lore; to try, in some way, to interpret what it (read: that being's existence) "meant." If anything at all. Over and over again in Dallas' work, there is that sense of survivor's guilt. As though the sole purpose of enduring through the drugs and the degradation was to be able to tell not only *her* story, but the stories of those who did not make it. Could not "get out alive," as it were.

Even the mighty megalodon, regarded as being among the most formidable predators ever to have existed on this strange (that is to say, fucked-up) Earth, could not persist, *survive*. And all that remains of the creature to make it "known" or "remembered" are the fossilized fragments that scientists (and even laymen) have found, including teeth. Indeed, the word "megalodon" means "big tooth." Whether or not Dallas intended to make that connection with this book's title, it applies to the fact that her writing style and preferred subject matters undeniably have some very big teeth. And yes, each one of Dallas' poems—with their evocative and time-spanning structure—feels like an entire storybook narrative (though not any kind of "bedtime story" one might want to tell their kids—unless to give an early preview of the horrors that life might [and will] have in store).

In poems like "If It Took Us Down Then, What About Now?" and "There Are Two Poems In This," Dallas is crystal clear about the brutality of losing someone. Particularly when it wasn't really "necessary," for lack of a better word. Of course, many (apart from just vampires) would argue that death is always unnecessary. However, in the world of hard living and fast dying that is so vividly depicted by Dallas, it seems especially to be the case.

To this end, the exploration of one's own lust for self-destruction is notably salient in *Megalodon*—almost like an admission to that old yarn about humanity having a death wish. One that the collective gets off on invoking and then managing to evade, at least for a little while (manifest in a line like, "Every day is/a death I/escape from" in "Sucker Punch"). After all, what sane (/non-rich) person would want to stick around to live in this shithole of a world? Failing death, the continued *risk of death* through numbing substances will have to suffice.

But for those who would try to say that Dallas "glorifies" drug use (and yeah, there are a lot of those conservative, oversimplifying types out there), ask yourself: is there any glory in being a "drug-girl" (another memorable poem title) or walking "to the pedophile's flophouse to get some coke"? No. It's just a way to exist when one doesn't quite adhere to another manner of "functioning." Particularly if we're talking about the aforementioned numbing benefits of *las drogas*. Even the "legal" ones that are more socially acceptable for housewives/soccer moms (as Dallas acknowledges in a poem like "Modern Wives Club," with the characterization, "They're on the Prozac and the Percs").

Even *they* can't help themselves with fretting over that pesky little thing called money. More to the point, the *constant concern* over money (whether wielding it to get one's next fix or not), which also relates back to that immortal adage from Richard Ashcroft, "It's a bittersweet symphony that's life/Trying to make ends meet/You're a slave to money then you die." Dallas' "Dollars" and "Ordinary Days" (detailing how "I am nothing so/busy keeping/up with/the

Joneses") both reiterate that "bittersweet" message, as she describes in the former, "I want to stop thinking about $/plagues me like it's a death." And while it might not "be" one, per se, it definitely drives a person to it as they engage in that soul-crushing thing called a paper chase when they could instead be using their mind for so much more. If money is a means to an end, Dallas phrases it better when she notes, "I am merely the means to my own end" in "Sucker Punch."

In another indelible poem, "One Day I'm Gonna Turn the Corner," Dallas pronounces herself to be a "Jane Doe" when her inevitable demise spurred by self-destructive, drug-addled tendencies arises. But that's not so for her readers, who feel as though they know her only too intimately with the absorption of each passing poem. And if you want to know something about "Jane Doe," know this: she "lived like a queen" and "died as a question mark." Like the megalodon itself. And just as we all will without a poet in our lives to immortalize the pain and suffering. To lend some meaning to it, even if only to turn the ugliness into misleadingly pretty words that bite with as much force and power as the megalodon's teeth.

Genna Rivieccio
Editor, The Opiate Books
Spring 2023

What I Wore to the Prom

I came out of the bowels of Queens
out of a suicidal mother
an alcoholic grandmother
pedophiles and touchers
a father who was not my father
bitches who would scar and scathe
boys who would hit and hurt
passersby would stare
shake their heads in sadness and breathe relief
since it wasn't their sadness
only mine inverted

I should have been a boy
I could have shoved and poked and maimed
instead of being the receiver
the recipient
the awardee
the homing pigeon
with the sign on my head
that read *losers welcome here*
(I could have escaped…)

but which cross was worse to bear
so I stayed
grinned
bore it
withstood
little by little
crawled out like a roach

kept going
when they threw rocks and blood ran

5

I kept going.......
they trailed behind
taunted and yelled
I kept on
I am free motherfuckers—free

years later
when this one died
of a heroin O.D.
and that one got her face pummeled in
during a crack war
the other one was found dead
and rotting in his car
I can keep going
(because there's a lot of 'em.......)

one has five kids
can't shake the syph
her abusive husband keeps riddling her with
one walked too far out onto the highway
on meth
rammed by an eighteen-wheeler
one's in state prison
for robbing a liquor store
with a shotgun
his three-year-old by his side
most are on welfare
living in the same hovels

I beelined out of
and this my dear is what we call
divine intervention
or just lucky as fuck.

Flashbacks

I.   1986
the Buick Regency
light blue with a dark blue
top, velvet seats
so plush
baby
it was a boat of a car
drove itself
down Cross Bay Boulevard
to Rockaway Beach 117
too much to drink
too much to snort
pulled over to vomit a blue wave
of Giffard Curaçao
the color of our interior
smoked a cig
recovered

II.   Headed south
to the beach
to sit under a silver
moon
slid over to me
on the passenger side
tried to love me
you were inoperative
defunct
dead
heard the waves crash
over and over
as the moon
magnetized the ocean
and we stared
like it was our end
as if this
were the last high
the last non-working play

III.   The Buick
our amphitheater
listened to the song
"When Doves Cry"
over and over
dawn beckoned
limpness cradled
you mumbled
it's okay I already knew
you shot up
listened to the waves
one more time with nothing left
but that damn hooptie
your cleft chin—devil within
as I always joked
even before the Buick
before dawn
before sexless desires
of powder and pills

IV.   Was so good to see the sun rage up
its rays blinded us to fainting
stumbled out to the mecca
you vomited again
I ran my hand over the sand
thought
this was so simple
never asked you for anything
yet it was a life sentence
and I just your sidekick
along for a death ride

I Bit the Hand

The hand that fed
clothed
held
smothered
the same hand that posed itself as comfort
fostered my birth

I chewed into the knuckles
they crunched and popped
ripped the hand off
shook it with rage
came back later to lick
down to bone

My savagery straight from the womb
or nurtured so off the spectrum
I was bled to believe
I squeezed out tainted
at eight I put a plastic bag over my head
to die
the hand did not remove it
at twelve I refused to cease screams
they fell dead under a muffled palm
the haunted sounds echoed backward
deep into my throat
bounced from rib to spine
caused a cataclysm

Later the hand settled around my esophagus
the same hand that dangled candy
slid me pills

questions were asked
where should we place her
what should we administer
fingers poked my eyes
pinched my lips to purple
I went dark
for years

Came back a savant
spoke in tongues
could not be decoded
sharpened teeth
loose cannon
not good around strangers
searched for the hand
later fattened with grief
from gorging on its tendons
I placed its dried-up remains in a jar
on clear days ponder as the bone dust
sparkles in the sunlight

Sister

Somewhere she is fat & pregnant & chained to her
ironing board
jelly-fat swishes around her buttocks / stretchmarks
spanning the map of
New Jersey creep along her belly & boulder breasts
her hair is filled with split ends & clumped together

like snakes on Medusa's head
She's waiting for husband #2 to come home with a
six-pack
of Budweiser & maybe
some money for milk & cereal

She's got a roach crawling up the wall & #5 up her womb
heavy as a heifer
she is still smoking Newports while #s 3 & 4
piss on the couch.......

11

Breaking Bread

Scene 1
Halloween
1985
I, in costume as a space alien
You, as a pirate
Us, high as motherfuckers
Traipsing up 6th Ave
Raveling ourselves within the parade
Weaving in and out of painted bodies
Glittered lashes
Elvira in drag
Twenty Michael Jacksons
Dracula and his coffin
Stop only to snuff—me
Inject—you
Hours
The tin man / cowboy / green wig girl
Limelight
I don't remember
Dawn came
At The Vault
I was pleasantly asked to pee on someone lurking in a pit
You were in the corner twitching
Sweat poured off you

Scene 2
Days later
Your ex knocked on the door
To leave your one-year-old son
In your care
While she hit up a rehab

I was concerned about your Rottweiler
Around a baby
You left for a four-day binge
I stole diapers
And used your cash
To get high
Not too high
Just enough
To carry on
With Lucifer
The Rottweiler
And your son
I realized the gold necklace
My godmother gave me was missing
You sold it to fund your binge
Rent was due
I never answered the door
Lucifer kept the landlord at bay

Scene 3
Halloween
1986
Me, your ex, your now two-year-old son
All of us dressed as Elvis
Your ex
Now a lesbian
In love with me
And completely rehabbed
Wants to spend every waking minute with us
(But really me)
I am only on the drink
These days
You search for more places to shoot up

13

Running out of smooth skin
We watch in disgust as you
Inject under your ball sac
I slur
While you lean on the wall
For hours
Beer bottles litter the apartment
Ex is frustrated
With our addictions
Threatens to take your son
And move back to West Virginia
Whispers to me
I can't leave you with him
He will ruin you

Pureland

I took brandy from the sitter I placed it to my lips my
tongue shrank
I kept to it I took the cigarette from your mouth
I took the needle pricked the vein I salved the sores
that festered between my toes and inside my thighs
I fought in the alleys and smoked the pipe I shared it
with whoever made it back I slept under the trestle I danced
ass cheeks out under a DJ screaming motherfucker
I prayed in a doorway escaping a rainstorm from
Mother Mary I crawled into a rancid bed that smelled—
I smelled
I turned you on your side to vomit out of your mouth
and not
choke to death I watched the stars with you sickened
with the HIV I confessed don't you know it
I told all until I was spent and reduced to a bug
I walked the bridge barefoot along the metal railing afraid
of nothing and if I fell off.......if I did........
I watched thieves murder the innocent and ransack
their belongings I picked through took this and that
I swallowed all pride turned myself over to foster strangers
to heal me to study me because
only the strong survive in this.......they want
to write about me what's there to say I've told it all
to that homeless clan who would listen in dead silence as I
coiled around them serpent-like with fascinating tales when
I ran through this city brimming with an insatiable thirst.......

Sucker Punch

Every day is
a death
I escape from
into a night
I know nothing about
I am merely
the means to
my own
end

There are Two Poems in This

The one about Brenda turning the leaf
and the other about Brenda dying
which came first
Brenda's death
or Brenda's turn?

I want to write a happy ending
I want to leave out
her emaciation
the fixes
the vomit-strewn trailer

Brenda my girl
had I not walked in to get my own fix
had I not seen you gray and foaming
and without any smarts—
cuz you know I was never very bright
I ran out screaming Jesus
to the pay phone
to hit 911
and scream into the phone
come quick she ain't breathin

I want to write something epic
but I fumble
all I got is shit

Brenda my girl
this is for you
this is for the boardwalk
at Rockaway

underneath with our blanket
our needles
our prayers
to our made-up water god we pretended
would save us from the waves
the incredible smile on your face when I found
that $20 bill

The second poem just can't birth
unless it oozes out
stillborn
cuz the second poem
haunts the first
yet I keep writing
as if I have something to say
if I listen so long to something
completely unbelievable
I will come to swear by it Brenda
I will

Po

Po River
that's the name yo
ain't none of yo business
what went down
or under
in that river
dark navy
slick sucked you in
got stuck there
day after day
joint after joint

We had nowhere else to go
but Po
River—been a meeting place for a hundred years
they said it's named after Edgar Allan Poe
cause some boy was serenading a girl right
at this very spot
at the river's edge where the wackaweeds tangle and knot
don't know what the scientific name is
we say wackaweeds 'cause you never knew what would
get washed up and tangled in them
like that girl who was serenaded with "To Helen"
looking out at Po
all starry-eyed
a hand drifted in
just a hand
slowly moving
heard that story for fifty years
girl thought it a hoax but
later there floated the foot
a cow's head
a yellowed pearl choker
things

19

stuff
pieces
caught themselves in the tangled vine
that bloomed purple velvet flowers
for most of the summer
flowers kept coming
ospreys soar overhead
people continued to
sit in the thick bed hoping
Po
would choke up something important

One-legged man will take you swamp fishing
through Po
into the reeds
fan boat on the oily
lukewarm with a brackish tint
he will light your cigarettes
tell you all this
tell you lovers come back every V-Day
say, with a hoarse cracked laugh
ain't venereal day
although that's a disease as thick as wackaweeds ova here
every Valentine's Day
some young lovers sit on the purple velvet flowers
believing they
gonna be different
from the lovers that came before them
while the ospreys feed their young
and we smoke
jay after jay
watch the water for stuff
floating in
that's gonna
get us money

Foraging

fuck give them a story they all want to know you tell them the time you hovered over the train tracks bone thin with the shakes out your ass and Barry Onter decided to take his life right then threw himself straight onto the tracks in a split second before the train came on him full speed rocked that motherfucker dead and all you could think about was what you could do with all that cash he probably had in his wallet you didn't get a chance to look through the wallet half his body was scarecrowed up on the train window and the other half dragged along the tracks into bits of pulp.......what can you say???? as you pour gin into juice to control the shakes this will most definitely get you through a potential relapse or collapse or perhaps you should just stop cold turkey like they did in the old days? why you gotta gin down a craving for a mad high I don't know but in the end you still a fucked-up honkey from Queens never had a chance at bum so story goes you got all strung out from crack you say fuck it get on Greyhound with your $148 you scavenged from your half-dead cancer-ridden grandmother you go down to Sanford—where was that? Florida? Where the fuck? Yep tell them how you met that stripper Lucrasia—was that her stage name? Jesus she was really played like she'd been run over maybe X-stripper but you two found each other and holed up in Mocahee's Motor Inn for days maybe weeks you were almost clean before then but she was using: a perfect combination of you + her = FUCKED and here you go again down the merry road of a lover of heroin of addicts of the dream the amazement the ahhhh fuck it and baby we miss you we miss the you that you once were but it ain't you no more and we can't accept those collect calls calling to collect money we can't give to users who still use when people dying on the tracks for nothing and you still going strong and able

If It Took Us Down Then, What About Now?

On the days when my only friend
came to visit her mom
her mom would clean herself up
they'd sit tight-knotted
table in between
and chain smoke

Later
after her mother left the table to shoot up
my friend would ring my bell
we'd head to the train trestle and sit
with legs dangled over the bridge
smoke all the cigs she clipped from her mom
we threw rocks at the top
of the freight train
as it whipped by
scream *motherfucker*
no one to see
hear us
or care

When we returned
we would find her mother
curled up in the corner
drool running down her chin

My friend would be on the juice by eighteen
and prostituting from the same
two rooms her mother crawled
through half-dead
to be carted out—half a veg
sent to another rehab

When we kissed
atop that weed-filled bridge
the train speeding so fast
under our worn sneakers
we didn't realize the electricity
that ran through us
charged our limbs
melded us together
as heavyweights
we just didn't see it
coming straight for us

Welcome to My Barren Womb Theater

I feel like a broke ass po bitch from a trailer park in
the Everglades I feel like I did when I was ten and Lisa
Sacristan picked
through my hair with a pen searching
for lice but it was just dirt and dandruff Lisa for the
record.......
I'm on a roll save me—save me from myself I ask
this sometimes when blood and guts ooze
out other times I'm dry as bone this time
1:04 a.m. in a town somewhere in the womb of the Gold
Coast I hear
the world is falling apart one scorched woodchip at a
time and I
can CNN or Google or Insta all the drama at any given
moment yet
I'm so caught up in my own little world of
make-believe the taxi driver's mouth dropped
open when he discovered I had no idea people died
in California or Oregon or wherever the fuck as
I'm too wrapped up in something called self-loathing and oh
yeah here is where I stop naturally but if I took it one
step—just
another step over the edge of confession—you'd understand
I am a selfish NYC bitch with angst
that dates back to
dirty hair dirty feet and yeah they didn't show me how
to wash how
to clean myself and when Lisa S. picked through my
hair I knew—I utterly
and completely knew how very imperfect—no no
that's not the right word—how

flawed
I really was and flaws root and flaws spread
like tumbleweeds through a desert and open up
into gaping balls of mental disarray yet I
pull it together so fucking perfect for eight to ten
hours a day claw at myself on the train home
monsters in my head monsters under the bed……..still there
at night—the boogeyman—I'm human I swear
I just want some quiet and enough mental focus to say
my last prayer for every creeping thing…….

Beastie

I wanted to write about those bitches
about how they followed me onto
the bus every day after school and spit
in my hair
about how they waited on my corner for me
to walk by and they hurled rocks at me
or chased me for blocks to cut me
to hurt

I was gonna put on paper how they crank called me
just to call me names
Slut
Lesbian
Dyke
Cunt

I was gonna admit that.......
yeah I stopped going to school
I stopped going outside altogether
and when they couldn't get at me
they would ring the bell and pleasantly call upon me
as if we were old friends
even study partners
but I wouldn't come out of my room

I was gonna say how it took a lifetime
to walk out the front door again and
I thought the passage was safe but they
no sooner found me and came at me
all of them

I wasn't sure if I should admit that I wished them
dead
every one of those ugly bitches
that bullied me because........well........
........I never actually knew why
I knew only simple things back then
the boys liked me
the girls liked me
I liked me
then I never liked me—or anyone—
again

after the first beating
when six girls jump on you and pummel
your face
you give up and pray to fade away into air

I was gonna say how much faster than me
I thought they were back then
much smarter
stronger
because they knew
I was a threat
and the only way to smite a threat
is to rub it out completely

A Story For My Villagers

I. This cold winter night
   stare out the window at stars
   at millennium
   stare until I turn foggy-eyed and think
   I got here—to this very spot
   torn and salvaged
   every wound scarred up—I got here

II. How I did it? There was no ordinary road
   surrounded by demons
   metal spoon cooling
   smell of Bacardi
   tobacco
   the pipes........oh the pipes

III. I can smell cocaine
   in any drugstore
   sense the added ingredients
   by rubbing the powder between my fingertips
   I still pine for one last stroll
   one last hurrah
   that consistent pining has become my diamond
   my life cord

IV. Naysayers will argue the rumor
   the mother of all stories of what happened to me
   back then
   ahhhh like childbirth
   I reprogrammed to forget any immense tidal
   waves
   that have shifted the flow of my body

or I would never have more children
what didn't rip me apart propelled me

V.   Not sure which demon sat its menacing
deformity in my crib
to whisper the atrocities of the world as I
lay dumbstruck
listening in curious angst
warned early on I would stroll
upon these, instead
I aimed straight for them
head on without blinders

VI.   The moment it all came to pass
that life-switch moment
near death
floating
oh baby I wanted to be taken
I awoke to face-slapping pain
carted off to I.C.U.
connected to I.V.
to the resurrection
to become a hideous
skel-crawl from an old and forgotten grave

VII.   Now I hold the universe in my hands
I see it and I try to follow it
the stars still here
old ones dead
new ones born
I stare at my nicked reflection in the window
a star in the sky wondrously sits
on my forehead

Drug-girl

Drug-girl rolls past
in the wheelchair
pushed endlessly
down bland white corridors
she longs to drool
half smiles at the other patients
droops her mouth down
in a saddened
feel-sorry-for-me way
to think she could have slid a few pills in
her hidey hole
and now this……

Mother and Father wait
obsequy statues
outside the MRI chamber
free from any potential radioactive
waves that could harm them
demand to know what's wrong with
drug-girl's brain
outraged that it has come to this
drug-girl waits
stares at the medical supply cabinet
gray-white faux wood
some kind of recycled board
shipped from a Third World country name of which
she could never pronounce
to end up
here
put together so half-assed, the bottom piece already
coming detached
cheap-ass shit

Drug-girl
perfectly still
when asked if she's ready
smiles
with dead eyes
what kind of music does she want to listen to
classical
dumb MRI bitches
don't know music
don't know drug-girl's struggles
in the morning
when she's sitting on the bowl
leveraging her fate with
whatever is left in
the bag
her goody bag
not so good when empty……

Or drug-girl's anger with that hideous supply closet
the hospital cheaped out on
Mom and Dad blame the millennial gen
the deteriorating school system
they blame each other's negligent malaise
over the years
their distraction away from drug-girl with
golf
yoga
glittery fundraisers
silicon boobs

Drug-girl is completely content
with how it all turned out
agitated that parents try to

reflect and
project the
would haves, could haves
she wants a burger she says
salty and ketchupy
like when she was a child
MRI bitch eyes her
Yeezys
David Yurman bracelet that she slides off
and places into
Gucci knapsack
drug-girl throws the
"I'll knife you"
stare

They gingerly
wheel her
to recently
renovated room 1011
with cushiony walls
drug-girl coils
around herself
stares at
nothing
thinks of
every
drug
she didn't get to

Homestead, FL

where your eye got plucked out in that awful
rumble
outside Zoomie's Bar
and you fought back like a banjee bitch
from hell
that ghetto girl plucked it like a grape from a vine
perfect
the pluck
not your eye
it was all yolk and glob
but it got you
money
from the state
so you holed up
in the Trade Winds Motel
the local pimp and his hookers
called you "Onesie"

when bored we would walk to Krome Avenue
to the pedophile's flophouse
to get some coke
once we sat on the steps of The Sanctuary
and partied under God's watch
you kept asking if it really was
a sanctuary
then the preacher arrived at seven a.m.
we were still sitting there as the sun rose
he took one look at your missing eye
and said Mother Mercy child patch that thing up

we moved on to the Everglades Motel
and I took up with the first sad case who asked
if I wanted to be in show biz and I said
yesssss
but it wasn't really (show biz)
tried to recruit you but you moved down
to Driftwood Trailer Park to shack up with a war vet
you said he suffered from Agent Orange poisoning
and heroin was his only saving grace
for such an awful affliction
I thought his orange hair was a direct reaction
(from the Agent Orange)
he got you an eyepatch with a skull on it
and that was everything to you
he told us these three points sum up life:
adopted kids are always fucked up
teachers are always wacked and
never ever trust a red-headed dealer in a casino

my pimp was stabbed eleven times
by some Russian in search of his missing sister
now I hit up the Last Chance Saloon
every night around eight p.m.
for exactly that
they are doing construction on
Steve Mainster Memorial Drive
and the preacher stands there
with a "Thank You Jesus" sign
and there you stand
and watch in sad remorse
as they pluck the dead palm tree
right from its socket of earth
and I think I know exactly what you are feeling

Sub-Divinity

There's that festering thing that
little regret / some little angst   can't put my finger on
it yet
it's always with me some form
of Satan under
my collar pressed against my bone at the base of
my neck
like a mole or a tag
when magnified one thousand times it's a
brutally ugly and distorted face I carry
cells that date back to the cross (did I throw
stones??.......) to a night in the desert
when I caved and I can't shake the enormous
burden of paying
the piper I could end it you know.......why
keep going when it's all Satan-bound anyhow
I will end up there again it's like a calling
try to resurrect my blackened heart
reshape it into a more compassionate heart—with
honor and patience.......sounds
boring as Satan laughs but my torn
soul is tired
temptation feels hauntingly played   I think I
want a new skin—I want to peel back my forehead
reprogram a thousand years of whoring
go home and bake a pie   wring my sickness
into that pie like Stephen King's *Thinner*—
let someone else eat it and
they in turn
take on these burdens while I stroll
away scot-free into the desert this
time an
angel

Dollars

I want to stop thinking about $
plagues me like it's a death
an end
shrouds any sense I could have had

Bills gotta get paid
I try to conjure up a genie
from this lantern
rub away at the
smooth brass carvings
they meant something
in another life perhaps
not this one
not this day
as I weep
impoverished

Rub my fingers together
feel a grainy scrape
no dollars appear
look to the clouds
bloated and gray
if I had a nickel or a quarter
for every knee jerk
every stomach drop
all the nicks in the road
if I could be that money whore
I'd be divinely rich

but one very sad
tramp

American Marriage

It's a cancer
that mutates and spreads
after rings are placed
on fingers
sacred prayers
bless us for eternity
it wove into the lace
of my dress
the knot of your bowtie
needled into our skin
blackened the grip between us
we sprout flagrant rants
(can we really be this pathetic?)
how quickly we rotted out
(your mother must have put a curse on us)
as just yesterday we held
our infant son
under the lazy sky and laughed
giddy like angels in flowerbeds
today you sit
gray as death
and plot my demise

Modern Wives Club

They're on the Prozac and the Percs
I am with them in body
in yoga
in Starbucks
in Candee's Nail Salon
we shop couture
we do lunch
we stare into space
then ooze into our Mercedes
sexting gym boys
hoping to secure the future
fuck of a lifetime
I can pop a few of those
pink-coated bad boys
I wouldn't mind
the zone for a bit
but I'm missing stuff
so I prefer to keep it real
because one day soon
I will long for that raw
laying-myself-down-on-the-bathroom-floor-and-
just-bawling-like-a-baby
emotion
Feel it
really feel it
my shrink says
I feel taller than a tree some days and
there are moments
when I prefer to roll myself under a moving bus
and let it all go to shit
but I wake up
clear-eyed
wildly aware
that I'm gonna die
no matter what
and someone
somewhere
in this house still needs me
even if it's just the dog

Withering Nymph

Buried deep in the womb of this soil
rolling around a dead
woodworm
I'm nested
eyes heavy with sleep

Yesterday
I brimmed with
the froth of youth
it burst from my breast
spewed stars
leaking galaxies

And I would wrap
eager fools into my folds

I rushed through them
with a windburn meant to sting

It didn't take a master of the universe
to spear a boy
it simply took a fire
that longed
to be stoked
over
and over

One Day I'm Gonna Turn the Corner

I won't be ready
never ready
on time
or prepared enough
the corner lurks like a menace
cracked and spindly

I'll tumble down
through a wormhole
without any water
or my phone
I'll have forgotten to bring
identification
splatter
onto the concrete

After they spatula me up
they'll dig through my pockets
find nothing

Jane Doe
lived like a queen
died as a question mark

Death by Dior #354

The beggar's curse
hangs heavy
over my chardonnay glass sans lip marks
as thunder cracks the silence
a shard of lightning so sharp
breaks this ball of Earth open
spills me into a long, long wormhole
all I can think about—as the storm sucks me in
is the lip gloss
I bought today at Dior
#354 SO LIGHT

So nude
the gloss was naked
made me blush when I applied it
so light it wasn't there

That beggar woman
she got so close to me
her rancid breath filled
with rot
she whispered in my ear
that tonight was my end
because I refused to give her
any money
that bitch pocketed
my new gloss

I don't believe
in hocus pocus
yet I pulled away quick

she lifted that damn gloss
while she sucked at my lobe
slutted me for my gloss—that nirvana
was the last one in stock
so tangy and sweet how it glazed over my lips

The rain on the roof so heavy
it snaps the Spanish tiles
while dry lips form
midnight approaches
my blank lips remain
as I segue into my flat lip death

Ordinary Days

Some days
I forget that
I am nothing so
busy keeping
up with
the Joneses
that other person
of blind wind
zipping through the
streets fast and crazy
have to get
to work
attend the meetings
the PTA
grocery store
gas
all the places I need to go
then something happens
the dog pisses
on the couch
my kid is failing in school
I find
heroin needles hidden
under the mattress
of my bed
and my
dead
heart
is bleeding into
my pillow
I come back
to me
to the
nothing that I
originally was

Megalodon

I started out
as the blindfish
sucked at soft particles
floated towards the warm spots
muddy and marked
felt your massive jaws
even before you clenched

I sifted through darkness
perhaps that was the gift
heard the crunch of poor creature's bones
their residue floated past me
I felt
never saw
and that was the gift

Once I brushed up
against your fin
you thought I was a parasite
invited me along to feast
with the many suckerfish
attached to your long
scarred body
I felt my way along your back
to your end
took me years
to separate feast from famine
fall back into nothingness

If I swam north
you swam north
south, south
again, invited to feast
better to live with my fear
than run the knots of the sea
in an endless escape

Still no sight as I nibbled
in all your nooks and crevices
I never could figure your size
never saw how colossal

I skirmished night and day
could have been chum
for any big fish
yet haunted by you
ocean to ocean
through the ice age
into global warming
still blind and boney
still bordering to end up
as a sea mate's gooey chum

Swim endlessly
always feel you close behind

Close-up

Look closely
see my veins
my lines
my coffee-stained teeth

how my heart wrenches
with every turn my children take
I long to live
to see their own kids
this want rooted so deeply into my
core it is an addiction in itself

Look closely
I'm aged
pressed into this life
like a cookie smashed in a jar
come closer
see the death line along
the inside of my wrinkled hand
yes this is me
close-up
and I'll dye my hair until
my fucking death

Acknowledgements

Donna Dallas wishes to acknowledge *Anti-Heroin Chic*, *Red Fez*, *Cajun Mutt Press*, *Beatnik Cowboy* and *The Opiate* for having previously published the selected works in this poetry book.

Donna Dallas' work has appeared in a plethora of journals, including *The Opiate*, *Beatnik Cowboy*, *Tribes*, *Horror Sleaze Trash* and *Fevers of the Mind*. She is the author of *Death Sisters*, her legacy novel, published by Alien Buddha Press. Her first chapbook, *Smoke and Mirrors*, launched in 2022 with *New York Quarterly*. Donna serves on the editorial team of *NYQ*.

CPSIA information can be obtained
at www.ICGtesting.com
Printed in the USA
BVHW030803110423
662129BV00014B/1417